Animal Behaviorists

BY ANNA-MARIA CRUM

Table of Contents

Introduction

If you could talk to animals, what do you think you would learn? Some pretty amazing things, probably! You might find out what they like to eat, where they like to live, and how they raise their babies. Animal behaviorists can't really talk to animals, but they study them to understand these things and many others.

Animal behaviorist
Joan Embery

Animal behaviorists also work to protect animals and animal homes. Animal behaviorists do their work in a variety of settings, from zoos to wildlife refuges.

In this book, you will learn about three animal behaviorists. Their work has made life better for the animals in their care.

Animal behaviorist
Kin Quitugua

Animal behaviorist
Ed Bangs

Joan Embery

As a child, Joan Embery dreamed of working with animals. But when she first tried, the few jobs open to women were filled. After nearly a year of trying, Joan was ready to give up. Just then the San Diego Zoo called her with an offer to work in the Children's Zoo.

Joan thought the job at the zoo would help prepare her to become a **veterinarian** (vet-ur-i-NAIR-ee-un). But she never left the zoo to study to be a vet. She stayed and became one of the best-known animal behaviorists.

Joan always wanted to work with animals. Here she works with a rhinoceros.

At the Children's Zoo, Joan spent a lot of time training animals. She also answered questions from visitors and made sure they didn't tease the animals. She fed and cared for the animals and kept their homes clean.

Most important, she made people aware of the zoo animals and their needs. In the past, children visiting the zoo were allowed to ride the Galápagos tortoise. Today, things are different. The health, safety, and comfort of the animals are the major concern.

It's a FACT!

The Galápagos tortoise weighs up to 600 pounds (270 kilograms). Its shell is 4 feet (1.2 meters) across. The oldest in captivity lived to be 152 years old!

Joan spent a lot of time training the elephants. An elephant uses its trunk to pick things up. It's an **instinctive behavior,** or a behavior an animal is born with. But an elephant first has to learn how to grab things on cue when asked by the trainer. This is a **learned behavior**. Joan used both types in her animal training.

When Joan trained the baby elephants, she used a special wooden cane. As a result of her training, if the bottom of an elephant's foot is tapped with the cane, the elephant will raise that foot. Just think how important that is to a handler if the elephant is about to step on his or her toe!

Animals must know the rules to survive. In Africa, a group of young male elephants started killing rhinos. The park rangers brought in older elephants to teach the younger ones some manners!

Joan poses with
a favorite condor.

Joan knows how important patience is in training wild animals. She also knows that although a trainer wants to win an animal's trust, the trainer must never trust the animal completely. When frightened, wild animals can easily forget their training. In that situation, the trainer must calm the animal so it remembers its training.

Some behaviors are common to a **species**, or group of very similar animals. Knowing these behaviors is helpful to a trainer. Joan believes that thinking like an animal is one of the most important things a good trainer can do. A good trainer shouldn't be frightened or overly confident.

Joan has given many talks about the zoo's animals, including some on television. She brings animals from the San Diego Zoo with her. She shows people the animals. To do this, she must know how to handle the animals safely. So she speaks to the keepers and works with the animals before she appears. She also reads books about animals.

Joan watches for signs that tell her what an animal is feeling. For example, when a dog is on guard, its ears point in the direction of danger. When horses and elephants are frightened, their eyes open wider and more white can be seen.

Joan once kept a tarantula on her desk for a week just to get over her fear of touching it.

Horses, sheep, two cheetahs, an aardvark, and a cougar are a few of the animals Joan keeps at her ranch. But she is quick to point out that they are not pets. Two dogs and a cat are her pets.

Joan spends some of her time working to protect **habitats** around the world. As part of a program with the Wildlife Health Center, she helps make people more aware of what it takes to keep animal habitats healthy.

Sometimes, Joan regrets not becoming a vet. But a vet usually sees only sick animals. Joan is lucky. She works with animals all the time and sees them at their best.

✔ Point

Make Connections

If you have a pet, what does it do to let you know it's happy or scared? Do your friends' pets act in the same way?

Kin Quitugua

Kin Quitugua (KIT-tu-gwa) is from Guam, an island in the Pacific Ocean. When he was nine, he saw a movie in which a trained hawk kills another bird while both are in flight. From that moment Kin knew he wanted to work with hawks.

When he was a child, Kin moved to Colorado with his family. Later, as a student in college, he met Rick Cole, a master falconer. A falconer is a person who is licensed to train and own birds of prey. Birds of prey are **predators**. They survive by killing and eating other animals. Kin asked Rick to teach him to be a falconer.

With training from a master falconer, Kin's dream of working with hawks came true.

Hawks, falcons, eagles, vultures, kites, harriers, and owls are **raptors**. Raptors are predators that use their feet to catch and kill their prey. A raptor's foot has four toes with curved claws called talons. The raptor uses its talons to grab and hold its food.

Birds of prey also have wings designed for their type of flying. Many kinds of eagles and vultures have long wings for soaring high in the sky. Kestrels (KES-tralz), a type of falcon, have pointed wings for flying fast.

It's a FACT!

Raptors have good eyesight. A kestrel can spot a grasshopper 300 feet (90 meters) away!

In order to keep a hawk, a person must have a license. To get one, a person must train under a master falconer and then pass a test.

Kin worked hard and learned all he could about raptors. He became a master falconer, and in 1986 he founded HawkQuest. Through HawkQuest, he brings many kinds of raptors to schools and other places for people to see. He lets the birds fly and teaches people about them.

Kin owns nine hawks, three eagles, four falcons, and eight owls. These birds can't survive on their own in the wild. They are hurt or have other problems.

Kin's favorite raptor is the Harris's Hawk. Unlike most raptors, they live in colonies with a female leader. Called the "Wolves of the Sky," they hunt as a group and share the kill.

Kin's raptors live in a structure called a **mews** (MUZE). In the mews the birds are tied to a perch in open wooden stalls. A shelf protects them from bad weather. Kin worries more about heat than snow. During long, hot summer days, a spray mist cools the birds. Sometimes a shade cloth is also used.

Volunteers exercise the birds. They attach a line from a bird's leg to a swivel, an object that spins around. The birds can fly in a circle, but they can't get away.

Point

Picture This

Reread the description of a mews. How do you imagine a mews looks? Draw a picture of your idea.

Forty volunteers look after Kin's birds. They feed and exercise the birds, clean the pens, and keep the birds cool.

The bald eagle nearly died out. But the efforts of animal behaviorists and others have saved it.

Training raptors is difficult. The raptors must trust a trainer before they can be taught. One of the best ways for a trainer to build trust is to feed the raptors.

Kin wears a thick leather glove on which he puts pieces of food for the bird he wants to train. He feeds the bird every day. Soon the bird connects him with food.

Kin also uses food to train a bird to fly on command. The bird rests on a perch with a line attached to its leg. Kin holds the line and stands three feet (1 meter) away. He puts a piece of food on his glove. The bird flies to the food. Kin does this over and over again. If he has done it right, the bird will fly to him when the line is taken off its leg.

Training takes a lot of patience. Kin has to get to know each bird well. What works with one bird may not work with another. Training birds never ends. Birds forget what they have been taught if the training isn't regularly repeated.

Last year, Kin spoke at hundreds of events across the country. He showed people how exciting birds of prey are and how interesting it is to learn more about them.

Kin weighs the birds every day. The birds won't fly unless they are hungry. Kin can tell if they are hungry by their weight.

15

Ed Bangs

Ed Bangs loves the outdoors and wanted a job that would let him work outside. So he studied wildlife management. In 1975, he went to work for the U.S. Fish and Wildlife Service at the Kenai (KEN-eye) National Wildlife Refuge in Alaska. He got what he wanted!

There, Ed did lots of things with animals. He put radio collars on wolves, studied brown bears, and **reintroduced** caribou. He also talked to people about living with wild animals.

In 1988, Ed moved to Montana to become project leader for wolf reintroduction in national parks in Montana, Idaho, and Wyoming. Reintroducing wolves was an important step toward keeping the wolves from becoming extinct.

Ed attaches a radio collar to a wolf to track its movements.

One of the first things Ed did as project leader was write an environmental impact statement, or EIS. This report had to answer many questions about bringing the wolves back. How would the wolves affect the local animal life? Would the wolves stay in their new homes? And most important to ranchers, would the wolves kill their livestock?

Not everyone was in favor of reintroducing the wolves. Some people in the area were against it because they feared attacks by wolves. Other people thought wolves were a natural part of the habitat and they were for it.

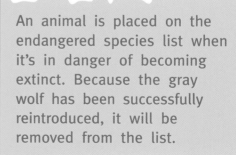

An animal is placed on the endangered species list when it's in danger of becoming extinct. Because the gray wolf has been successfully reintroduced, it will be removed from the list.

The EIS study led by Ed had to look at both sides of the question. Wolf packs hunt over a large area. It would be impossible to keep them within the national parks. The packs would come into contact with livestock. Understanding wolf behavior was important in figuring out what would happen then.

After all the questions were studied and answered, Ed's report was made public. It was in favor of bringing back the wolves. A wildlife group offered to pay ranchers for any livestock killed by the wolves. Everyone was satisfied.

How Wolves Talk

A wolf "talks" to another wolf by means of its body posture and tail positions.

Body in this posture when running says the wolf is playing.

Body in this posture when running says the wolf is afraid.

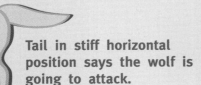

Tail in stiff horizontal position says the wolf is going to attack.

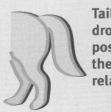

Tail in drooped position says the wolf is relaxed.

Ed now had to find wolves to reintroduce. He wanted to put family groups in Yellowstone National Park in Wyoming and young adults in Idaho. Wolves were already in Montana.

With permission from the Canadian government, Ed and his team followed wolf packs in Canada. Radio collars on some wolves helped the team locate the packs. In time they had enough wolves to bring back to the United States.

The wolves that were brought to Yellowstone were placed in **soft release**. This means the wolves are put in large pens for eight to ten weeks so they can get used to their new home. Ed used this method so the family packs would stay in the park area.

Even when the pen doors were left open for two days, the wolves didn't leave. This might have been because they did not understand that they could get out. After all, there are no doors in the wild!

Ed used **hard release** with the wolves in Idaho. The wolves were let go right away. In this way the young wolves form new packs.

At the very last minute, the Farm Bureau tried to stop the wolf release. Ed spent the night in an airport hangar among crates that contained the wolves. Finally, he received the telephone message, "Ed, turn them loose!" The wolves would have a new home in Idaho.

On January 14, 1995, Ed helped open the first crate. On the banks of the River of No-Return Wilderness, a gray wolf ran off into the distance. Everyone watched in amazement.

When a wolf is captured, it is first shot with a dart containing a drug that makes the wolf go to sleep. Then it is checked by a veterinarian and loaded into a crate for the trip to its new home.

In 2002, Ed and his team counted 560 wolves, including 200 pups. More than 100,000 people have seen wolves in Yellowstone Park. With the wolves back, elk and deer herds don't get too big. Because there are fewer elk and deer, aspen and willow trees can grow where they haven't grown for 70 years. The return of the wolves has made the habitat complete.

There are times in people's lives when they know they have done the right thing. Watching that first wolf run into the wilderness was this kind of moment for Ed.

Bounding out of its cage, a wolf returns to its natural habitat.

Conclusion

Understanding animals takes time, patience, and dedication. Those who work with animals must know what an animal is feeling and how to earn its trust. Animal behaviorists do these things. Hopefully, their work will help the world see how all living creatures are connected.

Biologists from Colorado are working in Mongolia to help save argali (AR-ga-lee) sheep from poachers. Poachers are people who kill or capture animals illegally. Argali sheep look like Rocky Mountain sheep, but are twice as big. They can weigh up to 400 pounds (180 kilograms).

Glossary

habitat   (HAB-i-tat) the area where a plant or animal normally lives (page 9)

hard release   (HARD ruh-LEES) releasing an animal directly from its crate into a new area (page 20)

instinctive behavior   (in-STINK-tiv bee-HAYV-yur) behavior an animal is born with (page 6)

learned behavior   (LURND bee-HAYV-yur) behavior an animal learns (page 6)

mews   (MUZE) the building where birds of prey live (page 13)

predator   (PRED-uh-tur) an animal that lives by killing and eating other animals (page 10)

raptor   (RAP-tur) a bird that uses its feet to catch and kill its prey (page 11)

reintroduce   (ree-in-tro-DOOS) bringing an animal back to its natural habitat (page 16)

soft release   (SAWFT ruh-LEES) keeping animals in a pen for weeks to get them used to the area before they are released (page 19)

species   (SPEE-sheez) a group of very similar plants or animals (page 7)

veterinarian   (vet-ur-i-NAIR-ee-un) a doctor who treats animals (page 4)

Index